This Strange Grace

poems by

Kelly Slivka

Finishing Line Press
Georgetown, Kentucky

This Strange Grace

ACKNOWLEDGMENTS

Thanks to *Alaska Quarterly Review* for deciding to publish "Forward" in
the Winter & Spring 2019 issue and to *Evening Street Review* for publishing
"What You Cannot Do" in issue Number 22. I'd also like to thank Waterford
Township Public Library for the unique opportunity of having a version
of "Eating Crow" featured in their Poetry Leaves exhibition and in the
corresponding anthology *Poetry Leaves: Volume 4.*

Finally, thanks to each special person in my life who has helped make the
action of creating this work possible. It takes a village to raise a poet, and it
likewise takes a village to enable poets to create poetry. Thank you for being
my village.

Publisher: Leah Maines
Editor: Christen Kincaid
Cover Art: Ryan Hubbard
Author Photo: Hans Hohl
Cover Design: Elizabeth Maines McCleavy

Printed in the USA on acid-free paper.
Order online: www.finishinglinepress.com
also available on amazon.com

Author inquiries and mail orders:
Finishing Line Press
P. O. Box 1626
Georgetown, Kentucky 40324
U. S. A.

Table of Contents

For those I love and those who love me.

LOMBOK

The driver takes me at dawn
along a thin highway
to the volcano's foot. From there,
a jungled trail steeps
to the rim.
I'm pregnant,
but I won't see it through.
Motherhood: out of black sleep
two eye slits into a mad
universe are cut.
The car rumples
along the shore before edging
inland, past skinny dogs with low-
pointed ears, white-rimmed sores, long
eyelashes. Past schoolchildren
laughing in pressed shirts
while they chafe their shoes
against the dirt.
On these islands
holy men bring gifts of
leashed goats and wing-clipped ducks
up to the sulfur-steaming calderas,
toss in their offerings to their gods.
My hands will go empty, my gifts
are unbearable.
As we near the trailhead
our speed steadies
with a motorbike.
On the back, a little girl
swathed in a crimson hijab presses
her head into her father's jacket. They
swerve around roosters and armfuls of
garbage, they push into air ripe with
sunshine and firesmoke, sea and
spiced prawns and waste.

The child's face is turned
away from me. What is it to live,
what is the offer, what is
the catch. She comes
of nothing, she leaves
with nothing, and
in between—

FORWARD

"What we call the future is a condition of increasing mess; what we call the past is increasing tidiness. Our ability to easily distinguish between the two shows that time in our world has a clear direction."
—Alan Lightman, "What Came Before the Big Bang?"
Harper's Magazine, January 2016

At 30 I came home and worked on a ski mountain.
This was last fall. I had been gone many years,
and my father had tired of work—would rather
tell me news of the owls nesting in our trees than
news of his business—and my mother had tired of
making meals—we always went out to eat—and
the valley roads had clogged with traffic. Each day
I drove up through the crevasses, up to the
whipped tips of the Rockies, a large and breathless
silence among the peaks, and I powered on
chairlift machinery, felt the steel quiver
in my teeth, watched the succession of chairs
swing past in endless, meditative monotony.
When no one needed a ride I took short circular
walks through snow drifts, up a little hill and down,
scouted ermine tracks and mountain hare, the crows
shiny black missiles in the bright sky, wary of my
lurching steps as I tamped down the thigh-deep snow.
Now and then I stopped to watch snow crystals blow off
spruce boughs in glamorous swirls, luminous, and I
foresaw how the ashes of my parents will move when
I cast them into the air above these peaks, who knows
how many years into the future. It is certain
they will die, and I will burn them. I long for the
meaning of that moment, long for the severance
life will provide as it takes things away from me,
always, year after year, proving its own maxim:

Decay will happen to everyone and everything:
The boulders will fall from the cliffside onto the road,
the oak bark will split, the land will slide from the hill
into the river and take you, too, if you're standing
there. And the only way to escape these collapses
is to live through them and put them behind you,
and the only way to live through them is to build
a good life that will one day collapse.
This is why I have circled back home to watch the
chairlift spin, to guide my feet through the snow,
to listen for the owls at dawn with my father and
cook dinner now and then for my mother. I want
to live well enough to survive the countless undoings.
The world is going forward, no matter what, us
tucked in with it, farther into the wilderness, thickets,
brambles, marshes, the past at our backs brighter, easier,
criss-crossed with trails. Now and now, tidier.

FIRERINGS

Do you know what
annealing is? It's the
strengthening of metal
through heat
and pressure. Heat

and pressure. July
is dry, windscorch
and crackle and
everyone fears fires—
we think we see

sweeps of smoke
on the valley floor
some days but it's
thick throats of haze. Do
you know I've moved on

from each thing
I've grown to love,
onward, as if it's the holy
quest, the inner sanctum:
the ritual, the praxis of

onward. I'm in love
again. Loosening
of cottonwood cotton,
limber aspens, tall grass
lists in the gusts. He has

warmth that rounds
wander into *wonderment*
and yet I can't
but consider how
we can always

say *no*. I've done
it so many times,
unburied myself
from the hearth
coals and squelched

out. Do you know
why we turn
away from these fires?
And step from their
rings into the night.

AFTER A FUNERAL

The flocks of daisies nesting
on these high hillsides mean
summer recedes again: Late

bloomers. Under the cool, clean
sun they ruffle their petals, they
bounce. They live their brief

apogee. Down in the cities
my friends' parents are dying,
in the heart, in the bone, in

the mind. Sometimes they're
told two days which turn into
two years, sometimes two

months which turn into two
days. One time a friend said
to me—while his father was

still here, still listening, while
the words were still possible—
said, *There are things I wish*

I could tell my father. We
cannot sidestep so many
of the tragedies we see

coming. These daisies will
not survive into winter, and
no one says what he means

at a deathbed. We cannot
make it through these motions
without meeting our losses—

of daisies, of dearests, of daylight.

AND ALMOST EVERY MOMENT

A sense, under the pale fists of clouds, the snowflakes
coming slowly as if they don't care to the ground
or wafting off to never fall at all, of languishing.
The institutions languish under their own obsolescence.
The poplar buds languish under winter's glaze of ice.
The browned grass languishes underfoot.
The will languishes under its oppressors.
And yet, the new hand offers itself out to be shook.
And yet, on the far rims of the fields, peach peals of light.
And isn't the tickle of wind on the boughs, the music
of the goose eggs hatching, like the human heart, perennial?

REVELATION, MID-STREET IN LONDON

This cyclist hurtles towards me, un-helmeted,
sport jacket, retro sneakers, at first a glint

in the yellow streetlights, then a credible threat,
and I—on vacation, crossing from Hyde Park

to The Swan bar—step up to avoid him then
back-step while he swerves one way then

the other, a panic-dance, and we cannot for the life
of us but implode into one another like two

planets pulled then pummeled in, the shock of it
after on my hands and knees quaking—

a small, mercurial moment and we are
eye to eye with our marrow, bodies owned

not by us but by the birth of the Universe—
our borrowed atoms coaxed apart,

rearranged and repurposed. We live between
the roughened palms of physics and

it is law: hemorrhage bone-bend skin-split
contusion concussion cavitation: these are the ways

we come to see ourselves as matter. Kneeling
in the street I survey myself, fingers

on each part, *Am I okay* but I can't say
surely in the warp of bloodrush before I lunge

at the guy, us both spitting-mad *What's your
issueYoucouldhavekilledmeWatchwhereyou'regoing.*

Outrageous and foolproof, our fragility. What else
makes us feel so alive? Sharpened steel, glottal

growls, a branch snapping in a dark
forest. Glimpses of our deepset orbits.

EATING CROW

I used to think you and I,
we don't deserve it.
But I've been wrong.

Sound of featherhush in wind as bird
heals low, flitter, shudder, shadow
on your eyelids, eclipse of

sun, rivertongue, smooth stone

in palm, levity and leniency
in your toss, the drop, a hollowsop
when the water yields then swallows

what you give it, leafbell, one
thin branch taps at another

and another, the aspen crowns

moan as they rub into each
other, Earthcreak, siltsuck—all of this

being here we do without
trying, this sensuous mess
we take inside—I thought us

unworthy, the gift inequitable.
Yet I've watched closely and
I see how there are

no tabs kept, no debts to pay. Life
demands no justification:

Coyote at scratch in every groundhole,
flicker in madhack for each fat grub,
wasp aswarm on the dead meat,
same as those, same as you—

I'm hungry, and each unearned
molecule, each brilliant sliver
of light I reap, I take, I eat, I keep.

THIS STRANGE GRACE

I spent a long summer at home with my parents
when I was too old to be spending summers at home.
So are you home from college? the gardener asked me,
and later the window-washer asked the same.
No. Cagily, side-eyed. *I'm 33.*

It was in fact my third return to the perennial nest.
Nothing would take—not work, not love, not direction.
I'd wrung my hands, driven back to Colorado,
sought asylum in mother's love and wallowed
in the shame of another formulaic failure to launch.

This was an erratic time.
I taught myself how to watercolor. I learned Spanish
from an old CD-ROM and practiced yoga from a cell phone app.
I didn't go into town much, didn't go to bars like I used to, to read
and drink and stare into the kaleidoscope of sports on the big screens.
I didn't want to meet anyone, to have to explain myself.
I didn't know how.
Instead, I watched time pass over the landscapes that had raised me.
The steep mountains, the piñons clinging to their sides.
The bare beige of early May, greener then greener,
the early darknesses becoming later and later.
Great horned owls floated around the tops of the ponderosa pines,
then kestrels, then Lewis's woodpeckers. The hummingbirds' whistles,
incessant, the Western tanagers appearing, then disappearing,
the rivers rising, then falling as quickly.
A flock of white pelicans high up like an armada of kites.
I think I mean to say there were unexpected blessings,
or what was expected manifested as blessings.
The dog rolling mindlessly in cool patches of Kentucky blue grass.
The young bucks who tip-toed along the fence line through June,
when they simply stopped coming. Mom in the doorway
in her nightgown, floating into my room to say goodnight.
Dad hunched over the kitchen trash bin, eating cherries.

The wind hooked through the valley floor in July,
building until in the afternoons it galed louder than the
Atlantic grinding against shores I had known back East.
It keeled through the loose green willows, the aspens trembling.
Cottonwood cotton clotted the window screen frames,
coated the cobwebs.
The damp soils gave way to chalky dirt, the fecund spring grasses
burnt out in the high sun, grew crisp. Come August, a haze
of wildfire smoke and dust lay gently in the air.
Something about a strong and steady wind
makes it hard to think, to act. I took guilty naps,
made too much coffee, gazed out, listless, from the back porch.

September arrived first on the highest peaks, up where the granite
meets the soils, the aspens coming into their yellows, oranges, reds,
the sound of them papery rather than lush. The colors moved
slowly down the hills into birches and wax currant bushes to meet me
along the riverside. I dug out my heavy jackets. A first frost.

Change is catching.
As the sun sank and shortened its stay in the day,
I felt the need to move. I found work
in another town, collected my things and headed out
over the graying hills in autumn sleet and falling clouds.
Was glad to go, relieved of my embarrassment, my sense of flailing.
Haven't gone back.

And yet, I often yearn to return to that place,
to fall asleep in those achy, airy afternoons with the juniper
branches ruffling on the hill behind the house, hiding in my room,
the bird sounds austere in my empty mind, the windows wide open.

I am not sure whether I want to say that in the drab corners
of life there floats a beguiling apparition of beauty, or that in the
constant wonder there can be only an apparition of drabness.
I mean to say we cannot but be here, always.
I mean to say grace falls upon us like light.

SUNDAY SONG

It's Tax Day, a warm day and a perfect
partly-cloudy, sun-soft evening.
I walk the path along the mountain
river, which is low for this time of year.
Some robins have returned—I can see
them through the still-bare trees—
and the mallards have paired up already.
They wheel in twos about the eddies.
Earlier, I arrived home after a long trip.
I got out of the car and went to check
on the back gate, it looked open, but
I saw it was properly latched, and when
I glanced into the yard I glanced
into two large, shiny black eyes: a flaxen
mule deer, lying down on the lawn, her
knees tucked under-chest. I haven't been
reading much lately, so I don't have any
words to borrow from others. I can only
compare her to what I know well, to my
same-old self. Her pink ears, my cupped palms.
Her legs thin as my forearms, brittle-looking
as my naked elbows. She stood, her eyes
wet as my tongue tight in my mouth.
She floated over the fence like a loosened
strand of hair drifting off in a breeze.
Her movements, sinews of muscle and slip
of bone under a rough pelt, a fluid blood
under my skin. What else do she and I share,
besides everything. Two versions of the same
story. Two strings called to play a
couple bars in this same symphony.

TREATISE ON HOMINIDAE

> "Researchers found that inducing awe—say, by having people
> stand in a grove of tall trees—increased generosity."
> —Matthew Hutson for *The Atlantic*,
> January/February, 2017

Which begs the question—What are we?

Whomever it was who first called us *Earthlings*
    in some shabby-chic sci-fi storyline

had it right, we are the fruit of the Earth,
        perhaps first, perhaps foremost, some chainlink

in an incredibly intricate and pointless unspooling.
    Incredible: (adj.) too extraordinary and

improbable to be believed, which is how we got our
        gods. Argue if you want, but I'm certain, this

is a mind decided. We came out of physics,
    which is surely not to say reason

but also, importantly, rules out magic like that
        found in storybooks and lore. We came out of

time and energy, rules and chance and un-ruminated
    ritual: birth, death, and the great, inexorable

truth: change. And it all happened right here
    on this knot of lava, rock and dust, the

species coming and going like the snows and the
    saunas of heat, like the sun day by day,

year by year, century, millennium, epoch, era,
    all that time in your cells, your bones, your

hair, your blood. All of that time at the root of your
cortex, your feelings, your very thoughts.

So is it any wonder the wet shade and radial
crown of a tree induces awe, which falls from

our throats right down into our hearts? Is it any
strangeness that not all of us want a ticket

on the rocket ship, that there's such an illogical
fear of flying? Loosed in a grip of empty

space, bodies far off the ground, the ground
that made us, that makes us *us*, the ground

that we Earthlings in turn have made the Earth,
have made into countries and histories and

hierarchies, races, revolutions, precious metals, acreage
for sale. As I was once told by a woman, a

Master of the Arts, a purveyor of ideas, a teacher:
Consider the environment of human nature.

We could go to Mars, she said, *but we would take
human nature with us.* Human/nature.

Humanature. We are our world. Inextricable,
undefined: hand after hand, error after

error, the urgent repetition of a dream
every night as if new. Life has been called

an explosion, often a journey, a path, but it is more a
scratching down, an impulsive dog-like

burying of ourselves in our own scent, a re-learning
   for each individual this lesson of what we are—

And you know what, head bent back, looking
   at the uppermost branches, the sky, the

strange language in the colors and patterns of clouds—
   Why do you try to read them? You want

to know yourself. We look out at the world and
   we are looking inside, the farther out, the closer

in, back to the beginning, to our moment, to our
   meaning—*Mirror, mirror,* we ply, *I know*

you are but what am I?

AFTER THE CAR ACCIDENT

I wasn't there,
I was in the kitchen pouring
another cup of coffee when
my husband ran a red light, got t-boned
by an oncoming driver.
He called me from the
shatter scene, the asphalt and gutted axle and
the indigo of August mornings,
trembly, teary-throated,
I just got crushed, he said.
So I drove out there, went slowly,
was already afraid
of the ominous air,
of bad things happening.
When I got there I tip-toed out across the lanes
to him and saw his Toyota grill
in the median and the glass
and the oil and the gas
and the way it had all been ripped apart
as if that was what it always wanted
to do. I waited
while the tow truck winched in
and my husband knelt
in front of the old man with the right of way
who was still sitting in the driver's seat
of his totaled Subaru, the air bags
draped half-cocked down the windows,
who'd gotten sliced up pretty badly
by the safety glass. My husband sobbed,
said he was so, so sorry, and then
that old man's wife ran up crying and waving
her hands like *no-no-no-no,* and we moved off.
She was in a flower shop apron.
She hugged her husband for a long time.

Then she walked over to us, we watched
her come, and
she hugged my husband, said *It's okay,*
You take care, dear, you are blessed.
She took my husband's head between her hands and leant
her mouth close into his shoulder
and said the Lord's Prayer—
at least, I think that's what it was—
Hail Mary, full of grace, etc.—
we're not the types who pray.
And then we left, I drove him home.
And we didn't know what to think,
weren't sure what happened, it was
a haunting, like so many of the most
poignant things are, and like so many
other poignant things, we will never
know much about it.

DOWNSIZING

This may seem like a familiar story. The parents sell their capacious cottage on the city skirts in favor of keeping a little apartment downtown, a place long on views but short on storage, so I help them minimize. Late one night we sort through boxes and boxes of old photos, plucking out a few unpartable keepers, tossing the rest. I see my father in a sepia-toned large-lapeled sport coat on a Salzburg bridge, I see family reunions and fly fishing trips and fuzzy, poolside Fourths of July. I see my mother in a

red dress, faint smile, pregnant with my older sister on the rocks over Monterey Bay. It is 1982 and she is twenty-six. Between her life and mine, an inscrutable vacancy—if seven years ago I had a husband and a house and the confidence to have daughters, I can't imagine—don't have those things now, have tried some and traded them in for other offers—namely, for the freedom to change my mind. Yet I feel in my fingernails, my esophagus, in the space between my brain and skull a sense that I missed out, that

irreplaceable gifts have been irrevocably lost. I won't know if my mother feels the same thing in reverse watching my feral life unfold— my collage of ill-selected lovers, one-bedroom apartments and half-cooked careers—I won't ask her, would not trust her answers. We must be loyal to what we are, because

we can never be otherwise. I will never turn thirty with two little girls balanced on each knee or plan my sixtieth anniversary with a partner. This is destiny: It isn't coming to understand what will happen but

coming to understand what will not. The pictures we will not take, the albums we will not make. As we get through the boxes, canisters of Kodak film, folders of negatives and cheap Hallmark photo books pile up in the trash bin. We all say we feel

lighter, and it's true. There in the garbage, some of our niggling has-beens, once-weres and how-comes will decompose among the memories. We're still learning to be what we became.

WHAT YOU CANNOT DO

On my writing desk, I keep a magnolia bud, twisted off a tree
in spring four years ago. It is the size of an almond, still attached
to a piece of its woody stomata-studded stem. It is silkily furred,
the skin underneath now dried out and brittle, a piece of the
sheath broken, revealing inside the tiny, tightly-rolled papers
of petals that never saw the sun. I think it is good
to hold in your hand a thing you could never make, not if you
harnessed all your human ingenuity and had a million lifetimes
with which to hew, to fail, to create, to try again.
It is important to remember what you cannot do.
You are surrounded by magics you cannot perform.
I have the heart-center swirl of a broken conch,
a chocolate-smooth Ohio buckeye and three
Northern flicker feathers, too,
on my desk. *What is the point of a feather?* you must
ask. Then, *What is the point of a bird?*
It is important to ask questions
until you arrive at the ones you will never be able to answer.
There are so many unfathomable facts. A feather is pushed
fully-formed from the skin. A five-ton Ohio buckeye tree unfolds
from a seed you can set in your palm, each twig breathing
through tiny mouths in its bark. A queen conch might live her slow,
mysterious life on the ocean floor through ten presidential terms.
It's likely every object you've ever touched
was made from something made by the earth.
When I look up at the stars and know some of their names,
I sometimes think I am bigger than I am.
But to name something is not to conquer it.
Nor is to hold it.
I remember this with the magnolia bud in my hand,
helpless to conceive how it is made, or why.

WHY READ POETRY

I know I'm not doing myself any favors sharing this with you, and
You'll probably just go on as before, but most of what you seek
From this poem—is it perspective, insight, beauty?—you'll find by
Setting it down and paying attention to other things, small things.
Think of our lives, their richness. Think of the choice of where to
Go to eat and whatever urges you to open your eyes upon waking,
Saying *rabbit rabbit* for luck on the first of the month and *god bless you*
To a stranger at the end of a sneeze. Or the way aluminum house slats
Are made to look like wood ones and some cell towers are built to
Look like trees, or the fact we have a Census Bureau, and it calls on the
Landline. Think of how the air is never completely still and the moment
Never completely silent, of how cars parked beneath birches in spring
Become covered by spongy red catkins. All this is telling you more
Than I ever could. Look up. You already have too much to consider.

As a general enthusiast of storytelling, **Kelly Slivka** has published journalism, videos, podcasts and interviews—while working on photography, fiction and essay projects—in addition to poetry. She obtained a Master of Arts degree in science journalism from New York University and received the Pearl Hogrefe Fellowship in Creative Writing from Iowa State University's Creative Writing and Environment MFA program.

Kelly's creative work has been featured in *Alaska Quarterly Review, Rise Up Review, TriQuarterly Review, Wild Goose Poetry Review* and elsewhere. She has worked as a features reporter for *The Daily Sentinel* newspaper in Grand Junction, Colorado, written for the Environment Desk at *The New York Times* and helped produce episodes of WNYC's Radiolab podcast series.

In other past lives, Kelly has been a professional ski instructor in the Rocky Mountains, a clerk at a liquor store, a barista and a purveyor of outdoor recreational equipment. After collecting a bachelor's degree in ecology, evolutionary biology and English literature from the University of Colorado at Boulder, Kelly left her home state of Colorado for New England, where she spent several years as a marine mammal ecologist. She worked aboard boats and planes crossing the Atlantic Ocean, studying whales, dolphins, seals and other protected species with various governmental and non-governmental research organizations.

Whatever her occupation and wherever she has found herself, Kelly remains a hiker, cyclist, sister, daughter, camper, reader, movie-goer, cocktail-maven and dedicated pet-petter, among other things. She can always be found online at kellyslivka.com.